Roger's Big Adventure:
"The Power to Never Give Up"

Cheri Marie Hand

Roger's Big Adventure:
The Power to Never Give Up
Copyright © 2025 by Cheri Marie Hand
All rights reserved.

No portion of this book may be reproduced or utilized in any form or by any means – electronic or mechanical, including photocopying or recording, or by any information storage and retrieval system – without written permission from the author.

ISBN: 979-8-9927763-3-1
Imprint: c'est cheri...

To Roger,

the most adorable, intelligent, spunky, sincere, sweet, dedicated and focused Parson Russell Terrier,

who continues to keep us in wonder each and every day - we love you!

Meet Roger – a Parson Russell Terrier!
Or as his friends like to call him,
"Roger the Russell"

Roger is very smart,
full of energy, and always very happy.

He knows what to do at the
right time, never gives up,
and
always thinks for himself.

Roger is brave and loves to explore. He's strong and always keeps going, no matter what!

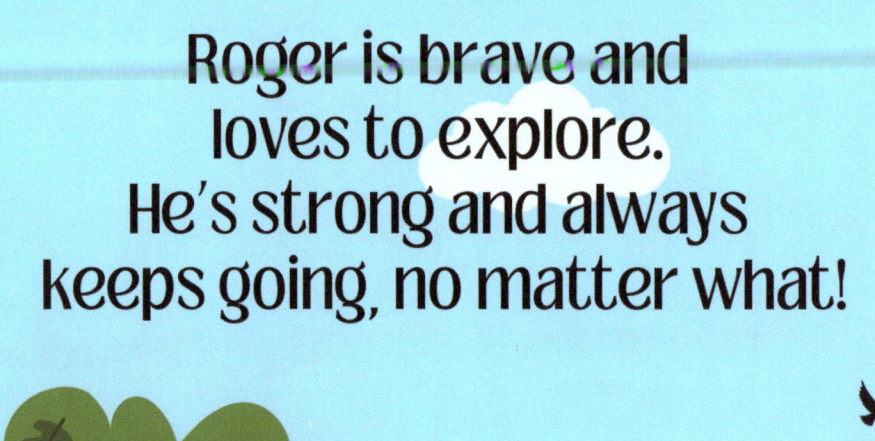

Roger really loves tennis balls!
He can't get enough of them...

Since the day he could walk, Roger has always loved playing catch!

If Roger could talk, he would say,
"I want to play with tennis balls
every day!
I love finding new tennis balls,
playing catch, and making up fun ball games
with my family."

Roger loves tennis balls.
Finding a new ball is always on his mind.
Because of his love for them,
he's learned to be strong
when looking for a ball -
even when things are tough.

Roger is learning to be Resilient

Roger has learned to keep going
and stay strong.
He knows if he is kind, curious,
and determined,
he can handle any challenge.

Roger loves an adventure!

Roger keeps his mind on the game,
thinking of smart ways to play.
When he needs a new tennis ball,
he finds one and keeps playing.
He's really good at getting his friends
to join in and have fun with him!

Roger may be small, but he's learning
no matter how tricky things get,
he can always bounce back - especially
with his friends by his side.

Roger starts every morning going on a walk with his mom and dad. Roger knows he needs his leash when leaving the house for a walk!

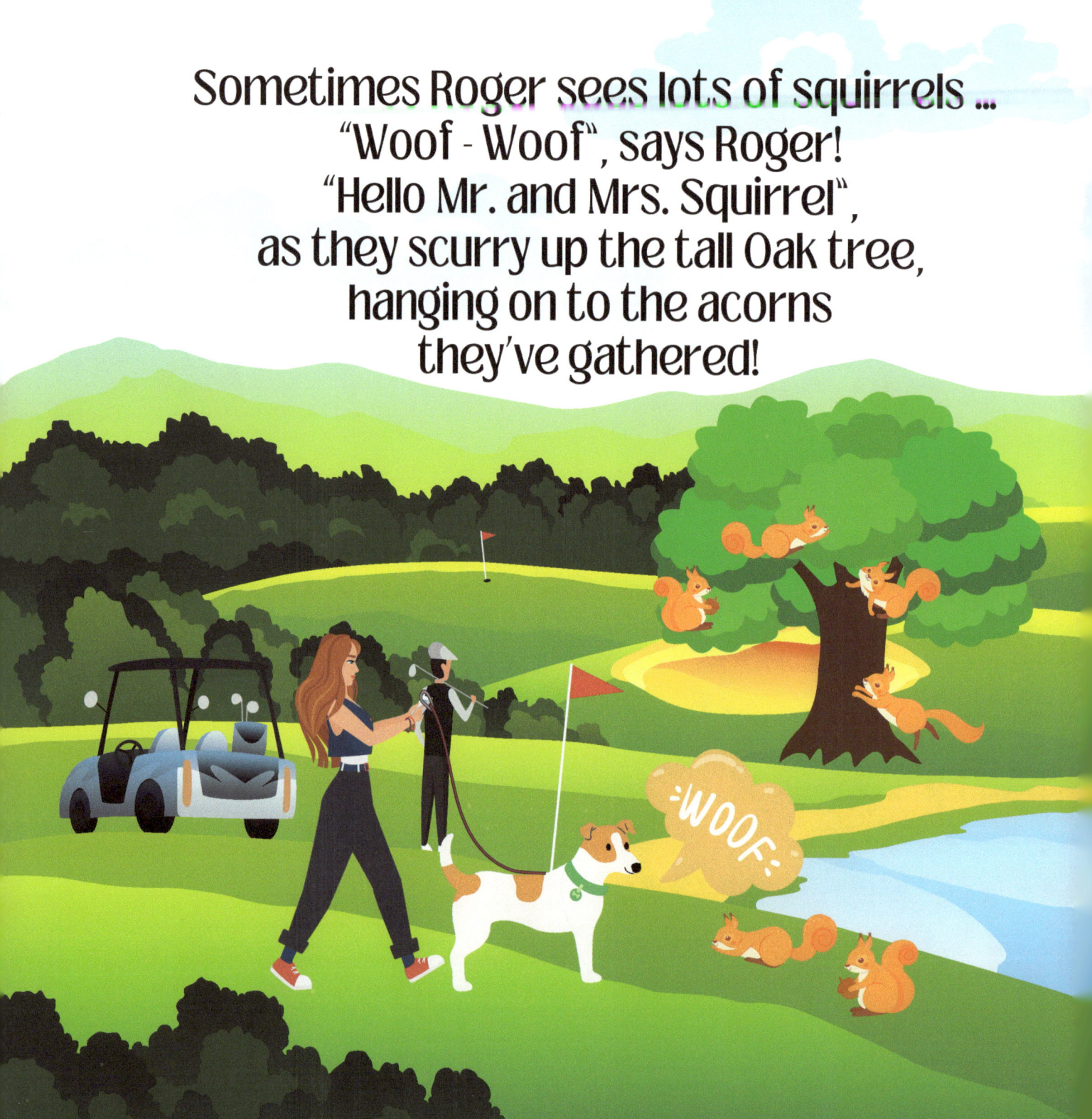

Sometimes Roger sees lots of squirrels ...
"Woof - Woof", says Roger!
"Hello Mr. and Mrs. Squirrel",
as they scurry up the tall Oak tree,
hanging on to the acorns
they've gathered!

Sometimes he spots the Deer Family quickly dashing about, as they are out for an early morning walk too - stopping to taste some flowers.
Papa, Mama and several baby fawn too!

Roger loves watching them waddle to the shoreline for a walkabout themselves!
"Quack - Quack"
they say to Roger!
Good morning to you too!

Roger also greets and says hello to the friendly Golf Rangers as they take out the golf carts for a busy day at the golf course.

Roger loves jumping in the golf cart too!

As Roger continues his adventure walk,
he spots a few stray golf balls.
Hmmm...he knows these are golf balls
which are very fun and challenging...
but not the same as a
bright yellow fuzzy tennis ball!

Roger starts sniffing and smelling under the bushes, flowers, plants and trees...

What is he looking for?

Lost and forgotten tennis balls, of course!
Sometimes tennis balls are hit
over the fence a little too hard and not
picked up by the players.
"These balls need a new home", thinks Roger!

Roger looks everywhere on the tennis courts - and in the bushes, flowers, and trees too! Sometimes he walks around two times! Roger knows he has to be really careful to keep trying to find more balls!

Sometimes Roger finds a tennis ball and sometimes ... he does not!

If today is not the day, then his mom and dad say - "Not today Roger- Maybe next time"

He knows he needs to be patient and figure things out while waiting for the next walk to try...one more time.

The best days are when Roger does find a tennis ball! He knows this will be a very special day!

When he finds one, he grabs the ball with his mouth and proudly trots down the sidewalk with his "prize"!

Mom and Dad are so proud of him and say, "Great job in finding a new ball, Roger!"

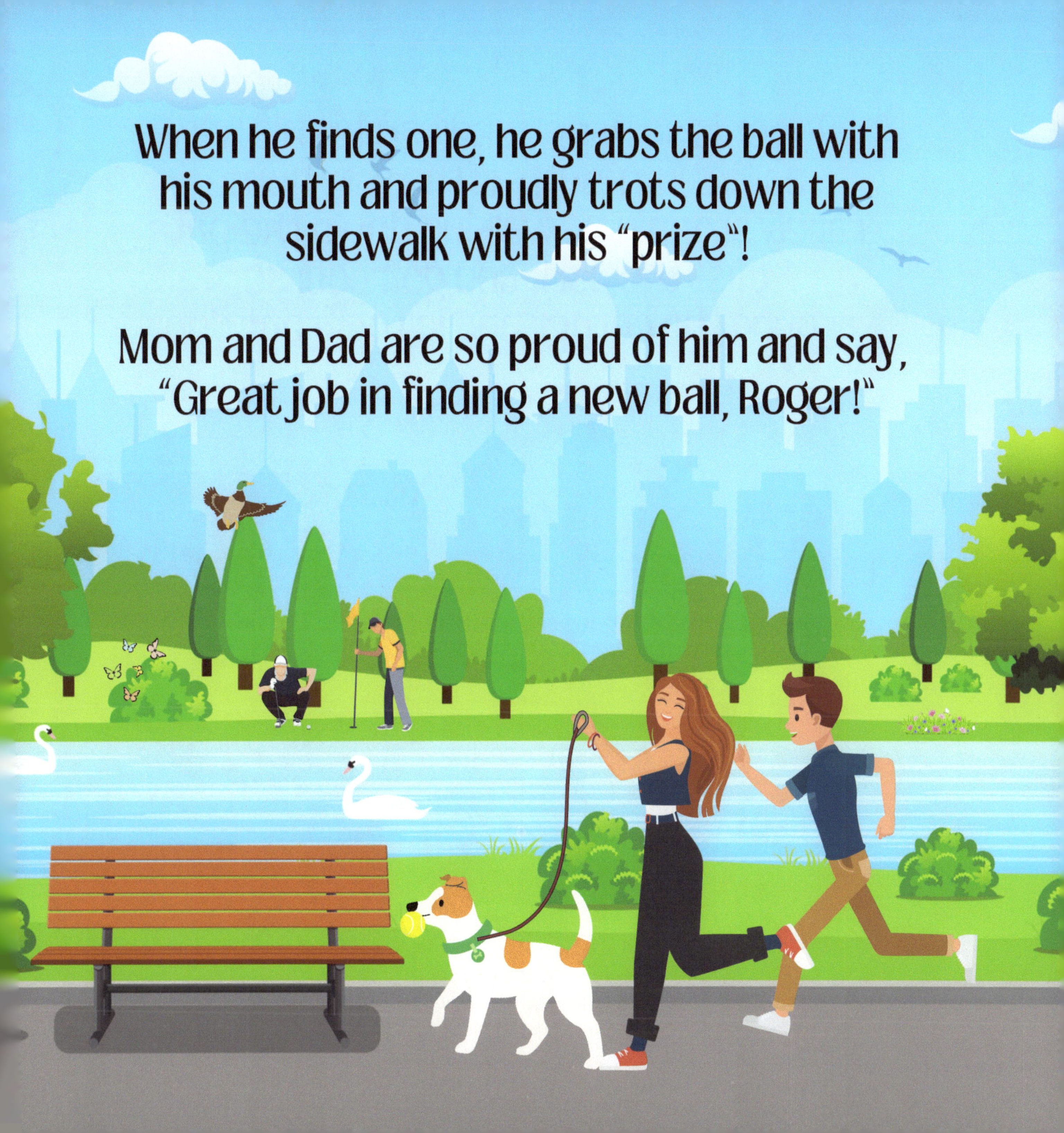

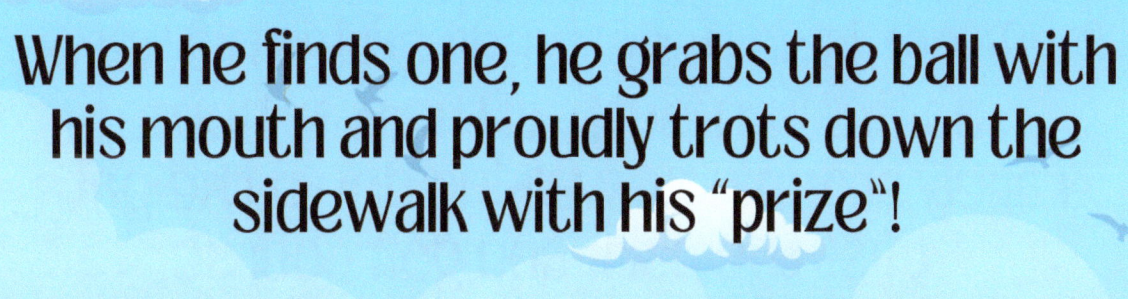

Now, Roger is ready to play tennis ball games!

He is very smart and loves creating new games -
Can you guess his favorites?

If you guessed some of these games,
you are right!
Staircase ball, Bucket ball, Standing Push ball,

And most favorite - Bath ball!

Roger remembers the most important part of being resilient -

the more he practices, the better he gets!

Being resilient means not giving up,
even when things are tough.

He knows if he keeps trying,
even when it's hard
(like when he can't find a tennis ball),
he will get better at it -
the more he looks!

He knows when he gets home, his basket of tennis balls are waiting for a fun day - still ahead!

With courage, confidence, never giving up, and a little luck - Roger will keep looking for more tennis balls on his next walk and be the happiest Resilient Russell

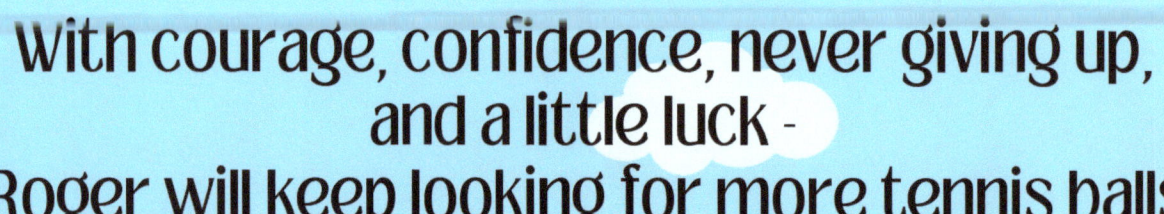

Join Roger and his friends
on more exciting adventures
as he keeps learning how to be a
Resilient Russell
and picks up other important skills too!

www.ingramcontent.com/pod-product-compliance
Lightning Source LLC
LaVergne TN
LVHW070440070526
838199LV00036B/671